I See, You See

JONAH AND THE WHALE

by Amy Bauman
Illustrated by MADA Design, Inc.

Meredith® Books
Des Moines, Iowa

God said to Jonah, "On a trip you must go! I'm displeased with Nineveh. The people must know."

Find the following:

2 black sheep 2 white sheep

gold coins 1 dog

2 shepherds 1 pitcher

2 butterflies 2 mice

1 shepherd's staff

But Jonah was frightened. He gave God the slip. Down at the harbor, he jumped 'board a ship.

Find the following:

2 seagulls

2 baskets of gold coins

2 dogs

1 hammer

4 soldiers

2 mice

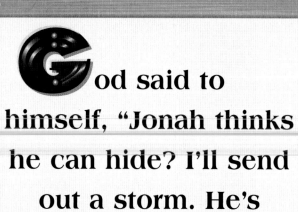od said to himself, "Jonah thinks he can hide? I'll send out a storm. He's in for a ride!"

Find the following:

gold

keys

 1 hammer

1 seagull

 1 mouse

1 island

 1 whale

 2 fish

 2 barrels

 1 rope

The ship tossed and turned on the angry black sea. "It's my fault," cried Jonah. "Please get rid of me." The sailors obeyed him—tossed him over the rail. But before he hit bottom, God sent out a whale.

Find the following:

treasure

2 seahorses

1 crab

2 boards

1 mouse

2 fish

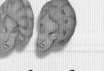

2 wooden faces

gold

In a gulp, there went Jonah. Down, down he went. Three days and three nights in the belly he spent.

Find the following:

1 sandal

2 turtles

1 crab

1 starfish

striped fish

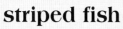

2 fish

3 coins

But God was still watching. He soon made things right. The whale spit out Jonah when land came in sight.

Find the following:

2 ducks   2 turtles

gold   1 sailboat   1 sandal

1 mouse   1 island

2 starfish   1 rowboat

YOUR #1
IDOL
SOURCE

IDOLS
FOR SALE

Out from the
waves to the shore
Jonah crawled.
"Jonah! To Nineveh!
I'm waiting,"
God called.

Find the following:

1 horse   2 sheep

1 pitcher   grapes   gold

1 mouse   1 whale

2 chickens   2 fish

YOUR #1
IDOL
SOURCE

IDOLS
FOR SALE

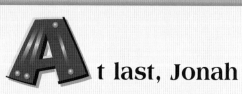t last, Jonah listened and did as God asked. He found talking with people was not a bad task. In the end, as was written, all came to good. "I am pleased!" the Lord called out. "All is as it should!"

Find the following:

2 musicians

gold

2 men

2 men carrying rugs

2 people praying

1 mouse

1 whale

2 baskets of flowers

2 butterflies

Flukes

WHAT IS THE LARGEST SEA CREATURE?

The blue whale is the largest animal in the ocean and in the world. Blue whales can grow to be about 80 feet long and can weigh as much as 120 tons. These enormous animals eat tiny sea creatures called plankton and krill.

HOW DO WHALES BREATHE UNDERWATER?

Whales are mammals just like dogs and cats and even you, so they need to breathe air just like you. A whale breathes air through nostrils, called a blowhole, which are often found at the top of a whale's head. While whales spend a lot of time under water, they have to come to the surface when they want to spout, or breathe.

Dorsal Fin

Blowhole

Flipper

THE STORY OF JONAH AND THE WHALE

One day God came to Jonah. "Jonah," God said, "go to the city of Nineveh. The people there have grown sinful. Tell them that their sinfulness saddens me."

Off Jonah went, but he did not go to Nineveh as God asked. Instead, thinking he could hide from God and the task God had given him, he ran to a nearby port. There he bought a ticket for a ship traveling to Tarshish, a country in the opposite direction from Nineveh. As the ship set sail, Jonah was sure he had outsmarted God. He thought God would never find him on a tiny ship in a big ocean.

But Jonah was very wrong. God knew exactly where he had gone. To prove this to Jonah, God sent a strong storm that caught the ship far out at sea. As the wind whistled and the sails flapped, the waves rose up, angrily tossing the ship around and around. The sailors were very afraid. They were sure the ship would be wrecked by the storm. Only Jonah, who had gone below deck to sleep, was unaware of the danger.

As the storm grew stronger, the sailors began praying. Again, only Jonah, who was still asleep, did not join in. When the shipmaster discovered him asleep below, he woke Jonah and told him what was happening. "Pray with us," he shouted to Jonah above the noise of the storm, "so that God might calm the storm and save us!"

Sadly, Jonah admitted that God might have sent the storm because of him. He told the sailors how he had run away from God rather than go to Nineveh as the Lord had asked. Now the sailors were even more afraid. Jonah told them to toss him overboard. At first the sailors refused, but as the storm raged on, they agreed.